SHAUN WHITE

The Flying Tomato's

Awesome Ride to

Olympic Gold

Sparkles McFun

1

Disclaimer

The following book is for entertainment and informational purposes only, for children. The information presented is without contract or any type of guarantee assurance. While every caution has been taken to provide accurate and current information, it is solely the reader's responsibility to check all information contained in this article before relying upon it. Neither the author nor the publisher can be held accountable for any errors or omissions.

Under no circumstances will any legal responsibility or blame be held against the author or publisher for any reparation, damages, or monetary loss due to the information presented, either directly or indirectly. This book is not intended as legal or medical advice. If any such specialized advice is needed, seek a qualified individual for help.

Trademarks are used without permission. Use of the trademark is not authorized by,

Table of Content

INTRODUCTION

Imagine being a superhero and taking off into the skies, landing flawlessly on a skateboard ramp or a halfpipe covered in snow. Shaun White is a legend in the snowboarding and skateboarding communities because he excels at doing just that. Shaun Roger White was born on September 3, 1986, in San Diego, California. He was raised in San Diego and had an amazing knack for these extreme activities early on.

Shaun's path to becoming a champion began in his early childhood. He was quite gregarious and enjoyed trying new things, particularly if they involved thrills and speed. When he was just six years old, his parents saw his spirit of adventure and brought him to the slopes to learn how to snowboard. Shaun thought he had discovered something amazing the first moment he stood on a snowboard. Despite his many falls in the beginning, he enjoyed the sensation of flying over the snow and was eager to recover.

Shaun had an interest in other sports outside snowboarding. He used his skateboard to cruise about his neighborhood when he wasn't in the snow. Using every curb and ramp he could find, he tried acrobatics and tricks to get the best of him. Shaun's first coach was his elder brother Jesse, who shared his passion for skateboarding. Shaun was inspired to persevere through difficult times by Jesse, who taught him many techniques.

Shaun's ability to overcome obstacles is one of his most remarkable qualities. He was born with a cardiac abnormality, so when he was little, he had to have two big heart surgeries. Shaun, though, wasn't deterred by it. Rather than backing down, it strengthened his resolve to follow his passion and excel as a skateboarder and snowboarder. At every stage, his parents, Roger and Cathy, drove him to tournaments and encouraged him while he trained.

Shaun began to compete in an increasing number of tournaments as he grew older. He took first place in a snowboarding competition at the age of seven, and by the time he was nine, a prominent snowboard brand had offered him a sponsorship. This indicated that he was already starting to be noticed for his talent and potential. Shaun didn't only participate in events; he won frequently and by a significant margin. Because of his brilliant red hair and amazing aerial talents, he was instantly dubbed "The Flying Tomato."

It was while still a teenager that Shaun got his big break. He made history in the Winter X Games, a renowned tournament for extreme sports, by being the youngest snowboarder to win a gold medal at the age of 16. His incredible career was only getting started with this triumph. Shaun became the most successful athlete in history to earn the most medals at the X Games. However, he didn't end there. His sights were fixed on the largest platform of all: the Winter Olympics. Shaun participated in his first Winter Olympics in Turin, Italy, in 2006. Shaun performed admirably despite the strain.

Shaun was unbeatable in the halfpipe event, where snowboarders use a U-shaped snow slope to execute flips and feats. He was flying over the pipe, swerving and twirling with amazing grace and dexterity. As he executed his last act, the audience erupted in cheers, and the judges gave him the gold medal. Shaun had won an Olympic gold medal, fulfilling his goal.

Yet Shaun didn't take his success for granted. He persisted in pushing the limits of what was feasible for snowboarding. He was often the first to try new techniques in contests, having devised them himself. Many young snowboarders have been motivated to pursue the sport by his unwavering passion and drive to be the greatest. Shaun truly pioneered the sport with his inventiveness and daring.

Shaun achieved success in sports other than snowboarding. Along with skateboarding, he gained notoriety by participating in and winning gold at the Summer X Games. It's an uncommon and amazing accomplishment for him to be a skilled snowboarder and skateboarder. Shaun demonstrated that you can excel in several areas with a lot of practice, hard effort, and commitment.

Shaun's cheerful demeanor and love of music are well-known outside of athletics. He picked up the guitar and even formed a band named Bad Things. Shaun's abilities are not limited to athletics; he and his band have performed at music festivals and recorded an album. Kids everywhere can be inspired by Shaun because of his spirit of adventure and readiness to try new things.

His narrative is one of fervor, tenacity, and pushing boundaries. He developed into a world champion and a beloved hero by many, starting as a small child who loved to skateboard and snowboard. His story shows us that with perseverance and hard effort, we can accomplish any goal, no matter how lofty. Anything is achievable if we believe in ourselves and never give up, as demonstrated by Shaun's amazing accomplishments and his thrilling experiences on the ramps and in the snow. Thus, keep in mind Shaun White, the young man who fulfilled his lofty ambitions, the next time you witness a skateboarder or snowboarder performing a breathtaking feat.

CHAPTER 1: THE EARLY YEARS

Shaun White's childhood was full of the type of thrills and adventures that would put a smile on any child's face. Shaun was a bundle of energy growing up in California; he was always on the go and always seeking the next adventure. Shaun's parents saw very clearly that he was not like other kids. Right from the time he could walk, he possessed an amazing ability to balance on any surface. Shaun was all over anything that could glide or had wheels.

Shaun was a little lad when it all began. Shaun wanted to follow in his elder brother Jesse's footsteps, just like any younger sibling would have wanted to be a skateboarder. He would be enthralled with

Jesse's acrobatics and tricks as he watched him skate with wide eyes. He decided to give it a go one day. Shaun rode his first down their driveway on a board that was nearly as large as he was. He staggered at first and fell, but he got back up and gave it another attempt. once more. once more. Before long, Shaun was skating faster than children twice his age.

Shaun, however, was drawn to more than simply skateboarding. His family visited the snow-capped Alps one winter. It was the most snow Shaun had ever seen in his life. The air was chilly and crisp, and everything was blanketed in a beautiful white blanket. Playing in the snow, his parents' modest cottage remained occupied during the days. Shaun was first exposed to snowboarding on this vacation. It seemed like skating in the snow as you saw others gliding down the slopes on boards. Shaun's eyes gleamed with anticipation. He pleaded with his parents to give it a go.

It was a beautiful first time for Shaun to snowboard. He had the same rush as when he rode his skateboard but added a whole new dimension of sliding on snow while strapped into a small children's board. Shaun struggled a little on the first few runs, but he soon got the feel of it. He was speeding down the slopes at the end of the day, grinning broadly. Shaun's new passion became snowboarding. He always looked forward to returning to the mountains in the winter, when he could speed down the fluffy hills and feel the blast of cold air on his face. Shaun's life at home was all about finding balance. as in really! He was always honing his craft. In their backyard, his parents constructed a little ramp for him to practice skating. He would practice new techniques for hours on end, falling a lot but always getting back up. He was a man of unyielding determination. When winter arrived, he would be riding his snowboard and attempting to perform skateboard tricks on the snow.

Shaun's formative years encompassed more than simply snowboarding and skating. He was an ordinary child who enjoyed playing with his friends, exploring new places, and challenging himself to reach his full potential. He had a brave heart and was always up for a task, no matter how daunting it appeared. His parents were the ones who supported him the most, telling him to never give up and to pursue his goals.

Shaun enjoyed viewing footage of snowboarders and skateboarders made by other people. He would spend hours observing their techniques and deducing how they pulled off their tricks. His goal was to become an expert in the sports he was passionate about. He would repeatedly rewind and rewatch the tapes until he knew every motion by heart. Once he could perform it on his own, he would practice outside. Shaun was insatiably curious and absorbed everything he saw and heard, much like a sponge.

Another aspect of Shaun's life was school. He wasn't always the best student; he would frequently daydream about going to the slopes or going skating. However, he was aware that academic success was as crucial. His parents made sure he took time for his hobbies and his education. Shaun developed good time management skills by making sure he completed his assignments before going to perform his stunts.

Shaun also participated in several tournaments throughout his formative years. Shaun enjoyed competing, whether it was in a neighborhood skateboarding competition or a fun sprint down the slopes with his brother. He loved a challenge and constantly pushed himself to do better. He gained confidence from these little contests and learned important lessons about winning and losing. He discovered that failing wasn't the end of the world—rather, it was an opportunity to grow and bounce back.

Shaun developed his skills as he grew older. He was starting to get recognition for his extraordinary talent in his neighborhood.

People would congregate to witness him snowboard and skate, in awe of this young man's abilities. Shaun stayed modest while enjoying the spotlight. He was aware that there was always more to discover and space for development.

It was only the beginning of his trip. The basis of what would become an incredible career was laid throughout his formative years. What made Shaun White the amazing athlete he would become was a combination of his love of the sport, the rush of the ride, and the satisfaction of learning a new trick. He had no idea that his exploits on the skateboard and snowboard were only the beginning of a remarkable journey that would propel him to the pinnacles of success and encourage young people everywhere to

follow their aspirations with the same
unwavering courage.

CHAPTER 2:

DISCOVERING

SNOWBOARDING

Shaun White was raised in San Diego, California, where the weather was nearly always sunny and surfers could hear the waves calling from a great distance. Shaun, however, was no typical child. He liked to explore new things and had a great passion for life from an early age. Because of his boundless energy and sense of adventure, he was constantly searching for his next great thrill.

When Shaun was just six years old, his family went to the Big Bear Lake's snow-capped mountains one day. His life will never be the same after this excursion. Back home, he had tried skateboarding and surfing, but snowboarding was a whole new experience for him. It was exciting and a little frightening to think about floating down a snowy mountain on a board, but Shaun was always up for a challenge.

It was weird for Shaun to strap into a snowboard for the first time. The boots were significantly thicker and the board was heavier than his skateboard. But something burned within him as he peered down the snow-covered slope. Shaun's father, who had always encouraged him in his crazy endeavors, offered him a hearty smile and a comforting nod. Shaun took a big breath, pushed off, and the journey started.

He stumbled and fell a lot at first. Shaun didn't bother that the chilly snow hurt his face each time he touched the ground. Every autumn was an opportunity to grow and improve. He got up repeatedly, brushed off the snow, and tried once again. His resolve was unbreakable. He gained confidence with each fall and eventually began to regain his balance.

Shaun found that snowboarding and skateboarding shared many similarities. He could also perform spins and flips on the snow, which were among the techniques he had honed at the skatepark. He became more and more enamored with the sensation of flying down the mountain, the wind whipping past him, and the earth appearing to be a blur as he practiced.

Shaun became hooked after the first day. Nothing had ever beckoned to him as the mountains did. He was on the slopes all the time, picking up new skills and challenging himself to go higher and faster. His family drove him to the mountains and encouraged him as he flew into the skies, supporting him every step of the way.

As Shaun grew older, his love for snowboarding intensified. He dreamed of the day he could snowboard like the world's finest riders as he studied the moves in their films. He practiced on a makeshift ramp in his garden when he was unable to get to the mountains, spending hours upon hours on the slopes.

Shaun started to stick out as he practiced. He dared to try pranks that most children his age would not have the courage to do. His technique was distinct, combining the fluidity of a surfer with the tricks of a skateboarder. People began to take note of the small child with flamboyant red hair who was able to perform almost impossible stunts on a snowboard.

One day Shaun got to compete in snowboarding locally and showcase his abilities. Shaun didn't care if the other opponents were more seasoned and older. Taking a deep breath, he propelled himself down the hill and amazed the crowd with a sequence of spins and flips. The applause was overwhelming as he flawlessly executed his last act.

Shaun not only won the race that day, but he also won the hearts of everyone who witnessed him ride. Nothing could stop him now that he had found his genuine passion. Shaun was prepared to put in more effort than ever to realize his goal of being the world's greatest snowboarder.

Shaun's reputation increased with each tournament he participated in. He visited several mountains, got to know other skilled snowboarders, and studied under the finest. Every novel encounter served as a chance for him to challenge himself and find fresh approaches to expressing his creativity in the snow.

For Shaun, snowboarding was an art form as much as a sport. Every leap was an instant of total freedom, and every trick was an opportunity to create a painting in the air. He enjoyed the adrenaline of flawlessly landing a new trick, the exhilaration of soaring high above the earth, and the sensation of his board cutting through the snow. He could be who he was and felt most alive when snowboarding.

Shaun's aspirations expanded along with his skill set. He dreamed of participating on the famous platforms of the Winter X Games and the Winter Olympics while he watched them. He was confident that he could succeed if he practiced and worked hard enough. His friends and family supported him and had faith in him, which gave him the willpower to keep moving forward.

Shaun had just begun her adventure into the world of snowboarding. Every new feat, every new challenge, every new peak was a step closer to his goal. He discovered that everything was achievable if you had passion, perseverance, and an unwavering heart. The world was about to see the heights to which the small San Diego child might fly after discovering his calling in the snow-capped mountains.

Shaun found snowboarding to be more than simply a sport; it was a way of life. It gave him lessons in tenacity, imagination, and the satisfaction that comes from pursuing your goals. And while he persisted in pushing the boundaries of what was conceivable on a snowboard, he motivated young people everywhere to discover their interests and aspirations.

CHAPTER 3: FIRST COMPETITIONS

Even as a small child, Shaun White had a wild spirit. He enjoyed skating around the streets and surfing the waves when he was a child in sunny California. But Shaun's entire life altered during a family vacation to the snow-capped Alps. It was colder than the concrete skateparks and warm beaches, but the snow was exciting. Instantly enthralled, he experienced the sensation of surfing on snow.

Snowboarding was another pastime of Shaun's elder brother, Jesse, who he aspired to emulate. His idol was Jesse, who never failed to impress him with his amazing stunts and rapid descents. All that Jesse knew was something Shaun wished to know.

Shaun started by practicing on a hand-me-down snowboard that was far too large. That was not simple. He was adamant about continuing despite falling frequently and becoming buried in snow.

After realizing Shaun's enthusiasm for snowboarding, his parents decided to encourage him in his endeavor. For him to practice, they frequently brought him to the mountains. Shaun became noticeable very quickly. His inherent skill and courageous attitude belied his considerable age and little stature compared to the other children. His first competition didn't take place very long after that.

It was nerve-wracking and thrilling for Shaun to compete in his maiden event. Comparing himself to children considerably older and larger than him, he was only seven years old. Shaun, though, didn't feel fear. It was time for him to prove his worth. Looking down at the course with its many jumps and hazards, his pulse raced as he stood at the top of the slope. He inhaled deeply before pushing off and beginning to run.

His speed and elegance as he descended the slope took everyone by surprise. Even though he was little, his confidence came from years of experience in his movements. He sprang through the air and landed with ease, hitting the leaps precisely. Bewildered by this small child with such tremendous skill, the audience sent out a loud shout. Shaun had a big smile on his face after finishing his almost faultless run.

Unexpectedly, Shaun emerged victorious in the inaugural contest. Beating more experienced opponents was quite an accomplishment for a small child, and Shaun possessed a unique talent. His confidence skyrocketed after the victory. Seeking to push himself to the limit, he was determined to continue snowboarding.

Shaun continued to participate in tournaments after his initial victory. Every experience offered a fresh opportunity to grow and learn. Though he never gave up and always had fun, he occasionally won and occasionally lost. He always felt supported by his parents and brother, who were there to encourage him no matter what. Upon entering the Junior Nationals, Shaun had one of his most memorable competing experiences. Many young, skilled snowboarders from throughout the nation participated in the large-scale event. Shaun was worried and excited at the same time since the competition was tough. He felt prepared, though. Day by day, he was improving, picking up new skills, and practicing a lot.

Shaun shocked everyone by demonstrating his improvement during the Junior Nationals. Impressing both the judges and onlookers, he performed amazing feats. With astonishing dexterity, he landed after spinning in the air and flipping his board. With his amazing runs, Shaun moved to the top of the leaderboard. He succeeded in winning. It was a major turning point in Shaun's early career to take first place. As far as snowboarding goes, he was among the finest of his generation.

Shaun found great success in these early events. He learned how to remain composed under duress, maintain his focus, and always challenge himself to do better. Snowboarding was Shaun's passion, along with the rush of competition. He had an almost weightless feeling each time he got into his board and headed to the slopes.

Shaun established plenty of friends in the snowboarding scene while he competed and won more races. He was talented, and the other students liked his laid-back, amiable demeanor. Shaun loved to have fun, cheer others on, and offer advice. Sharing a passion for snowboarding with a community was something he cherished.

Sponsors were also drawn to Shaun's competitiveness. After spotting his skill, snowboarding equipment manufacturers asked him to endorse their goods. Shaun could now get the greatest gear and assistance for his snowboarding escapades, which made this a huge thing. Moreover, it indicated that even at this young age, he was becoming a professional athlete.

Throughout every tournament, Shaun's passion for snowboarding remained constant. His boredom with it never grew. A fresh chance to learn something new and have fun awaited each day on the slopes. Shaun had to work hard, be very determined, and experience a lot of joy to go from his first competition to winning. Even at such a young age, he demonstrated that everything is possible if you have desire and persistence.

Consequently, Shaun White's status increased with every tournament, both in terms of altitude and metaphor. It was exciting to watch where this young snowboarder with potential would go next because his adventure was just getting started.

CHAPTER 4: RISING TO FAME

The amazing story of Shaun White's ascent to prominence is one of skill, perseverance, and a passion for exploration. Shaun displayed a natural talent and an endless curiosity from the minute he strapped on a snowboard, traits that would later propel him into the spotlight. His family frequently had winter holidays in the snow-capped Alps, which is where his narrative starts. When Shaun started snowboarding for the first time at the age of six, he fell in love with the activity right away. Shaun was not like other kids his age who would have been happy to merely slide down the hill; instead, he wanted to be an expert at every turn, jump, and spin.

There were many victories and falls during his early days on the slopes. Shaun understood that every fall he took was a step closer to learning a new skill, therefore he didn't fear falling. Other snowboarders and coaches noticed the little boy's bold demeanor and recognized something unique in him. He possessed an extraordinary capacity for fast learning, pushing himself to the limit, and rising from failures no matter how severe. Shaun's parents were ardent supporters of his enthusiasm. They saw his potential and supported him in following his goals, even if it meant logging many hours behind the wheel to train in the mountains. Shaun was constantly moving, whether it was in the water, on a skateboard, or in the snow, so much so that his father used to make jokes about him being half monkey and half fish.

Shaun started competing in regional events as his abilities increased. These were tiny events, but they provided Shaun with an ideal platform to display his developing skills. Soon after he started to succeed, rumors about the teenage snowboarding prodigy started to circulate. Shaun's triumphs secured him sponsorships, which were essential in enabling him to intensify his training and compete in larger events. But Shaun's ascent to prominence involved more than merely triumphing in contests. It also had to do with his distinct style and contagious enthusiasm. Known as "The Flying Tomato," he proudly sported his long red hair. He was well-liked by both spectators and rival athletes due to his lighthearted nature and passion for the game. He made snowboarding seem like an absolute blast, which is why people liked to watch him.

Shaun's 13-year-old year was his big break. He met the requirements to compete in the Winter X Games, a renowned competition that drew the top snowboarders from across the globe. Shaun held his own against much older and more seasoned riders, even impressing the judges with his daring stunts and polished style. Despite not winning that year, he had left his imprint. Shaun's profile kept growing in the next few years. He participated in further X Games and won prizes and medals in the process. His unwavering will to excel led him to consistently innovate and put in more training. Shaun was constantly trying to push the limits of what was conceivable on a snowboard by learning new techniques.

Shaun competed in the Winter Olympics, fulfilling one of his greatest aspirations at the age of 19. With the entire world looking on, the pressure was tremendous, but Shaun handled it well. He put on an incredible show in the halfpipe competition, landing things that nobody else could. With a virtually flawless last run, he won a gold medal and cemented his place in the annals of snowboarding history. Shaun's victory at the Olympics increased his notoriety. He became a global role model for aspiring snowboarders after making appearances on television shows and magazine covers. Shaun maintained his modesty and devotion to his passions, snowboarding and skateboarding, despite his notoriety.

He wasn't content to only snowboard; he also became well-known for his skating. He demonstrated that his skill wasn't just for the snow when he competed in the Summer X Games. His achievements as a skateboarder demonstrated his flexibility as an athlete. Shaun is a great sports hero because of his extraordinary accomplishments in both snowboarding and skateboarding. Shaun used his platform to give back in addition to his sporting accomplishments. He visited children's hospitals, gave to charitable causes, and encouraged a great number of young people to follow their ambitions. Shaun's tale serves as an example of the strength of perseverance, hard effort, and devotion. He demonstrated that everything is achievable if you have passion for what you do and perseverance.

His ascent to popularity is a brilliant illustration of what you can achieve if you have faith in yourself and never give up. Shaun's journey from a small child on the slopes to a worldwide celebrity is one of bravery, adventure, and aiming for excellence. Around the world, fresh generations of snowboarders, skateboarders, and visionaries are still motivated by his legacy.

CHAPTER 5: OLYMPIC DREAMS

Olympic aspirations for Shaun White resembled a crazy roller coaster trip with lots of turns, twists, and beautiful moments. Picture yourself at the summit of a massive snow-capped mountain, your heart thumping like a drum and the icy wind piercing your cheeks. For Shaun, this was the beginning of an incredible journey rather than simply a dream.

Shaun has always enjoyed moving quickly. He felt at home whether he was snowboarding through the snow or skateboarding down a hill at top speed. With a wide smile and even higher goals, he was a daredevil. The Olympics provided him with an ideal platform to showcase his abilities to the globe, including the greatest athletes in the world on a huge scale.

When Shaun was barely a teenager, he experienced the Olympics for the first time. Imagine a sea of people, athletes from all over the world assembling, cameras blazing. Shaun was prepared to outshine everyone in his ability to soar higher and spin more quickly at the Winter Olympics. He had spent years developing his craft and executing seemingly impossible stunts.

Shaun was anxious to leave his imprint as he went into the snow for the Winter Olympics in Turin, Italy in 2006. His playground was the halfpipe, a huge U-shaped ramp dusted with snow. Reaping the thrills of exhilaration mixed with dread, he stood at the top and peered down the cold walls. He turned into a speeding, colorful blur as he plummeted in, soaring through the air with amazing flips and spins. As Shaun performed trick after daring trick, the audience gasped in amazement.

And then it took place. Shaun won the gold medal when he executed his last performance flawlessly. It was him! He had won an Olympic gold medal. What made it so remarkable, though, was not so much the gold as it was the satisfaction of performing what he loved in the international arena. Numerous children were motivated to dream big and have confidence in themselves by his contagious zeal and extraordinary skill.

Shaun's Olympic career, however, didn't stop there. He returned four years later, this time to Vancouver, Canada. Shaun was prepared, even though the competition was tough. He was prepared with a covert tool, a maneuver known as the "Double McTwist 1260." It was an incredible maneuver, comprising two flips and three and a half spins, something no one had ever seen before. He kept it for last, and the fans went crazy as he nailed it perfectly. Shaun wins again another gold medal!

There was more to Shaun's accomplishment than just medals. It was all about continually trying to be better and pushing the boundaries of what was conceivable. He practiced for hours on end, falling and climbing back up while continually setting his sights higher. His path wasn't simple. Shaun had setbacks and injuries, but her resolve remained unwavering.

Shaun was a seasoned veteran by the time the 2014 Winter Olympics in Sochi, Russia, came around. He had to contend with some of the world's top snowboarders, though, as the competition was fiercer than ever. Despite his best efforts, he was not awarded a medal this time around. Even though Shaun found it difficult to swallow, she persisted. He understood that failing served as a springboard for achievement.

Shaun set his sights on the 2018 Winter Olympics in Pyeongchang, South Korea, determined to return stronger. He exercised more diligently than ever, straining both his body and his mind. Shaun realized that the Olympics might be his final opportunity to compete internationally. He was resolute despite the tremendous pressure.

Shaun was prepared on the day of the halfpipe competition. With a combination of power and grace, he soared through the air, skillfully landing trick after trick. As he got ready for his farewell run, the audience held its breath. Shaun had to do something amazing because the gold medal was on the line.

Then he carried it out. Shaun started his last trick, an amazing series of flips and spins that had everyone in awe. The crowd cheered as he touched down. Once more, Shaun had done it! With the win of his third Olympic gold medal, he cemented his status as one of the all-time great snowboarders.

His aspirations for the Olympics went beyond merely winning medals. They were about chasing his passion, overcoming obstacles, and inspiring others to follow their dreams. He showed that with hard work, dedication, and a fearless spirit, anything is possible. Whether on a snowy mountain or a skateboard ramp, Shaun

White's tale is a testimony to the power of
dreaming big and never giving up.

CHAPTER 6:
SKATEBOARDING
SUCCESS

Shaun White's story resembles a thrilling skateboard ride with lots of turns, twists, and amazing leaps. Imagine a small child with a bright smile, a heart full of hopes, and a wild shock of red hair. That youngster is Shaun White, and it has been nothing short of incredible to follow his path to become a skateboarding icon.

California, where Shaun was born and raised, is renowned for its sunny climate and excellent skating locations. He had a deep affinity for movement and speed from an early age. Shaun was constantly moving, whether it was skating, riding his bike, or climbing trees. He had a lot of energy and was constantly seeking out new tasks.

Shaun once witnessed some older children performing skateboard tricks at the neighborhood skate park. With amazing talent, they were flipping their boards, spinning in the air, and riding down ramps. Shaun became enthralled. He observed their every move for hours. He was certain that he wanted to resemble them.

Shaun's parents eventually bought him a skateboard after much pleading. Before long, he was spending every day at the skate park honing his tricks and striving for improvement. He stumbled a lot at first. Gaining proficiency in skateboarding requires a lot of practice and skill. Shaun persisted nonetheless. He always got back up and tried again after falling. He was committed to growing and learning.

Shaun began to improve as he practiced. He picked up the skill of ollieing, or jumping with your skateboard and lifting it off the ground. Then he picked up the art of kickflipping, in which you land in the air and the board spins beneath your feet. With every new trick he learned, his confidence and enthusiasm for skating increased.

Nobody failed to notice Shaun's abilities. His ability began to be recognized by fellow skateboarders and even by some professional skateboarders. They were astounded by his fearlessness and how rapidly he picked up new skills. Shaun was already participating in and winning skateboarding events by the time he was a teenager!

Shaun's talent wasn't the only factor in his success, though. He put in a ton of work. Every day, he dedicated hours to practicing, always challenging himself to improve. He viewed footage of skateboarding stunts, researched other skaters, and even created his routines. His commitment to the game and his enthusiasm for it were incredibly motivating.

Shaun's big break came when he began participating in the world's greatest skateboarders and snowboarders, who compete in the X Games, a major extreme sports event. A medal at the X Games is an enormous accomplishment, as it is comparable to the Olympics of extreme sports. Shaun took home gold medals in addition to regular medals! He gave amazing performances. He performed feats of skill that were previously unheard of and made them appear simple. He was adored by the audience and rose to fame as a skateboarder.

Shaun's inventiveness was among the many unique qualities that set him apart. He didn't merely perform the same stunts as other people. He created new ones and infused whatever he did with his style. He was constantly coming up with new ideas to push himself and add excitement to skateboarding.

Shaun's success as a skateboarder has also contributed to his status as an international role model for youth. He demonstrated to them that great things are possible if you put in the necessary effort and pursue your goals. He gave a lot of young kids confidence and the motivation to start skating.

Shaun's path wasn't always simple, though. He occasionally experienced injuries that required him to stop skating. Sport-related injuries are common and can be quite difficult to recover from. But Shaun maintained his optimism despite his injuries. During his recuperation, he planned his next movements and came up with new techniques. He never allowed failures to deter him from going after his goals.

Shaun eventually rose to prominence as one of the world's most well-known skateboarders. He broke records, won several tournaments, and gained widespread recognition. Due to his ability to make skateboarding appear thrilling and joyful, people enjoyed watching him. He became known for his red hair and wide smile, and he was always excited to meet new people and share his passion for skating with them.

Shaun's prowess as a skateboarder gave him a lot of possibilities. He had his video games and has acted in movies and TV series. In addition, he collaborated with skating businesses to develop his brand of equipment and skateboards. Shaun never lost why he initially started skating, though—he loved it—no matter how well-known he grew.

His tale is a fantastic illustration of how enthusiasm, diligence, and persistence can result in extraordinary achievement. He demonstrated that everything is possible if you have a desire and a lot of perseverance. Shaun saw skateboarding as a means of self-expression, pushing boundaries, and having fun rather than merely a sport. And for that reason, he became a genuine skateboarding icon.

CHAPTER 7: OVERCOMING CHALLENGES

American former skateboarder and snowboarder Shaun White has an amazing tale of overcoming adversity. Similar to the hills and ramps he conquered, his path is full of twists and turns, ups and downs. Shaun had to overcome challenges from an early age that may have prevented him from being the legend he is today, but his tenacity and enthusiasm carried him through.

Shaun had a severe medical problem called Tetralogy of Fallot, a cardiac abnormality when he was a little child. This illness necessitated surgery. Imagine going through something terrifying as a young guy! Shaun, nevertheless, didn't let it deter him. He was able to go through it because of his resilient nature and his loving family. Though he had to exercise caution and heed the doctor's advice, his dreams of snowboarding and skateboarding never ended.

Shaun had an early passion for adrenaline sports. He would try to emulate his older brother Jesse's antics by observing him. His parents took him to the slopes one day so he could try snowboarding. He was hooked right away. However, snowboarding isn't simple, particularly for someone who has recently had heart operations repaired. Shaun suffered injuries from falls regularly, yet he never gave up, constantly striving for better. Falling was only a part of the process, he realized, and every fall brought with it a new lesson.

Shaun wasn't the largest or strongest child in school. Occasionally, he was mocked by other youngsters because of the way his operations had changed his appearance. But Shaun remained unaffected by what they said. Rather, he concentrated on his passions, which were skateboarding and snowboarding. Whether it was in his backyard on a handmade ramp or the icy slopes, he practiced any moment he had. He learned more and more skills, showing that his effort had paid off.

Shaun had more difficult obstacles as he grew older. Skateboarders and snowboarders faced the world's top athletes when they competed in these sports. Shaun frequently had self-doubt because of the tremendous pressure. He would ask himself, "Can I do this?" as he saw other contestants. However, each time such ideas surfaced, he reminded himself of his progress. He recalled how he had triumphed over the falls, the surgeries, and the taunting. He was aware that everything was possible for him if he continued to go forward.

Shaun faced a significant obstacle when he decided to compete in the Olympics. Since the Olympics represent the pinnacle of athletic competition, Shaun was determined to establish his superiority. However, the path to the Olympics proved difficult. He had to train more diligently than ever before, frequently dedicating hours to perfecting the same technique on the slopes. He had wounds, fatigue, and times of uncertainty. Shaun's resolve, nevertheless, never faltered. Shaun's perseverance paid off in 2006 when he participated in the Winter Olympics in

Turin, Italy. Because of his amazing aerial stunts and long red hair, he had already earned the nickname "The Flying Tomato". Shaun had challenging weather and formidable opponents during the competition. He missed a decent score on his first run in the halfpipe finals due to a fall. Shaun's spirit may have been broken at that moment, yet he persisted. Breathing deeply, he concentrated on his next sprint and threw himself into it. His incredible performance won him the gold medal and cemented his status as one of the world's greatest snowboarders.

However, Shaun's tale is not over yet. He persisted in challenging himself, taking on new tasks and always aiming higher. He had difficulties in the years that followed, including ailments that needed surgery and prolonged recuperation times. Shaun overcame these setbacks each time, emerging stronger than before. With the same fervor and resolve that had gotten him through his whole career, he accepted the fact that conquering obstacles was a necessary part of the path.

Shaun had to reconcile his passion for snowboarding and skateboarding with other hobbies in addition to his physical accomplishments. He started to play guitar in his band and was interested in music. Another obstacle Shaun had was balancing his career in music and athletics, yet he was able to succeed in both. He demonstrated that you can follow several loves if you put in enough effort by learning time management skills and maintaining focus on your objectives.

His narrative serves as a tribute to the strength of tenacity and will. He overcame several obstacles, such as severe competition and health problems, but he never let them stop him. Rather, he saw every setback as a chance to learn and advance. For young people dealing with their struggles, Shaun's story demonstrates that everything is achievable with perseverance, desire, and an optimistic outlook. Remember Shaun's narrative and have faith in your ability to overcome obstacles in life, whether you're falling off a snowboard or facing another challenge.

CHAPTER 8: THE LEGEND OF THE FLYING TOMATO

Shaun White, dubbed "The Flying Tomato" due to his long red hair, is a remarkable athlete who achieved amazing success in the snowboarding and skateboarding worlds. Imagine a child who enjoyed riding his skateboard fast, performing tricks, and having a good time. That was the start of Shaun's story. He was a typical youngster with a lofty aspiration.

Shaun, who grew up in California, fell in love with skateboarding at an early age. He enjoyed the rush of wind in his face as he raced through the streets, the thrill of trying out new maneuvers, and the satisfaction of pulling them off. Shaun's enthusiasm didn't end there, either. He went to the snow-capped mountains with his snowboard instead of his skateboard when winter arrived.

Shaun had a bit of a catastrophe on his snowboarding debut. He took a bunch of falls and became snow-covered. But he persisted in trying. He continued honing his balancing skills and improving daily. Soon, he was performing incredible stunts on the hillsides, just as he did on his skateboard. He was vivacious, brave, and driven.

People were aware of Shaun's extraordinary potential. He was good, period, not just outstanding for his age. He started competing and emerged victorious. Shaun started snowboarding professionally at the age of 13. It was obvious that he was unique, and because of his brilliant red hair and amazing acrobatics that allowed him to soar through the air, the moniker "The Flying Tomato" stuck.

Shaun was a dominant force in competitions, not merely a participant. At the age of fifteen, he took first place in the Winter X Games, his first significant competition. Winning an X Game is a significant accomplishment; these competitions are similar to the Olympics for extreme sports. For Shaun, though, this was only the start. He kept winning, breaking records, and expanding the bounds of what was thought to be feasible for snowboarding.

The halfpipe was one of Shaun's favorite events. Imagine a massive snow ramp that forms a U shape. Snowboarders would race up one side, fling themselves into the air to do tricks, and then come back down to repeat the process. Shaun came to the fore on the halfpipe. He has unique abilities to spin, flip, and twist. His acrobatics were so elaborate and lofty that they looked unreal, akin to something from a superhero film.

But Shaun's motivation went beyond simply winning. Because snowboarding was so enjoyable, he wanted to spread that happiness to as many people as possible. He turned into a global role model for children, demonstrating to them that they too could fulfill their aspirations through dedication and hard work. He never stopped laughing, smiling, and inspiring people to reach their full potential.

Shaun's greatest ambition was to represent her country in the Winter Olympics. The pinnacle of athletic performance is to win a gold medal at the Olympics, the most esteemed competition in the world. Shaun was given his shot in 2006. The entire world was watching as he headed to Italy to compete in the Winter Olympics.

There was fierce competition for the halfpipe. There were the top snowboarders from across the globe, competing with one another. But Shaun was composed and concentrated. He knew he was prepared since he had trained hard. He sprang into the air, flipping and twisting like a bird when it was his time. As he flawlessly executed each trick, the audience gasped. Shaun had taken home the gold medal when the results were in! He had achieved his goal of becoming an Olympic champion.

Shaun didn't stop there, either. He went on to compete and succeed. At the 2010 Winter Olympics in Canada and the 2018 Winter

Olympics in South Korea, he took home two more gold medals. Every time, he created new feats and records while pushing the limits of what was thought to be possible in snowboarding. He went on to become the all-time greatest snowboarder.

Shaun was gifted in more than just snowboarding. He was a skilled skateboarder as well. He participated in the X Games skateboarding competition as well, taking home trophies and astounding everyone with his abilities. He was even more remarkable since he was one of the rare athletes who could excel in two distinct sports.

Shaun has a good heart and was giving even away from the game. He took advantage of his celebrity to assist charitable causes and encourage young people to pursue their aspirations. In addition to starting his own business and producing snowboards and skateboards, he also picked up the guitar and joined a band. Shaun demonstrated that with hard effort and self-truth, one can excel in a variety of fields.

Shaun's narrative is one of tenacity, enthusiasm, and good times. He demonstrated that incredible things are possible if you have a big idea and put in a lot of effort. He became known as "The Flying Tomato" and a legend in the snowboarding and skating communities as he soared into the skies like a bird. Not only does he have amazing talents, but kids all around the world look up to him because of his good attitude and enthusiasm for what he does. Shaun White will always be known as the young guy who achieved great heights,

followed his ambitions, and won the hearts
of many.

CHAPTER 9: LIFE OFF THE BOARD

The off-court adventures of Shaun White are equally captivating as his on-court exploits. In addition to snowboarding and skateboarding, he engages in a range of other hobbies that highlight his diverse skills and passions. For Shaun, life is about embracing new experiences, pursuing aspirations, and changing the world, not simply about competing and taking home medals.

Shaun is great, and his love of music is one of his best qualities. In addition to being an avid music enthusiast, he possesses musical skills. Shaun is a guitarist who performs in a band named Bad Things. Shaun can express himself artistically in a new way since he plays in a band. He likes to compose music, rehearse with his friends, and play live for an audience. Shaun loves music and finds it to be a great way to relax and have fun.

Shaun's passion for adventure plays a significant role in his life. Shaun enjoys traveling and discovering new locations when he's not practicing or competing. Shaun is a game for an adventure whether it takes place on a sunny beach, in a busy metropolis, or in a peaceful mountain hideaway. He likes socializing with new people, sampling cuisine, and taking in the splendor of many civilizations. Shaun finds that travel keeps him inspired and serves as a constant reminder of how vast and varied the world is.

Shaun enjoys starting and operating his own company since he is an entrepreneur as well.

His successful business endeavors include the apparel brand WHITESPACE. Shaun's apparel collection is a reflection of his distinct and stylish aesthetic. He takes pleasure in creating clothing that is not only fashionable but also cozy and useful. Shaun has learned a lot about endurance, hard work, and inventiveness since launching his own company.

Shaun is a big believer in giving back to the community. He feels that he should use his fortune and notoriety to better others. Shaun has participated in several humanitarian endeavors, such as working with the Make-A-Wish Foundation, which grants children with life-threatening diseases their wishes. Shaun enjoys getting to know these children, learning about their lives, and witnessing their joy as their dreams come true. Shaun finds great satisfaction and delight in helping others.

Shaun is a well-known athlete, but he also appreciates the little things in life. He values his time with friends and family greatly. Shaun enjoys spending time with his parents and brothers, who have always encouraged him in his professional endeavors. In addition, he likes to unwind at home, watch movies, and play with his pets. Shaun finds solace in these experiences, which serve as a constant reminder of what's important in life.

Many others find inspiration in Shaun. His transformation from a young child with lofty goals to a well-known athlete inspires us to value grit and diligence. Shaun frequently talks about his experiences and inspires people to pursue their dreams and persevere no matter how difficult life may seem. His unwavering optimism and tenacity inspire us to believe that everything is possible for us if we put in the necessary work and have faith in ourselves.

Shaun's curiosity and openness to trying new things are among the qualities that make his life off the board so fascinating. He doesn't hesitate to take on new tasks and leave his comfort zone. Beyond snowboarding and skateboarding, he has pursued a variety of interests and pastimes due to his sense of adventure. Shaun's life is fascinating and full of surprises since he is open to trying new things.

In Shaun's life, balance is also important. He exercises hard and puts in a lot of work, but he also understands the need to look after himself. Shaun maintains his physical and mental well-being by engaging in mindfulness and relaxation activities. He makes sure to take time to unwind and rejuvenate since he recognizes that rest and recuperation are equally as vital as exercising.

Shaun's appreciation of the environment is another facet of his existence. Shaun grew raised in the highlands and has a strong love and respect for the natural world. He is engaged in several environmental initiatives and recognizes the value of preserving our world. Shaun utilizes his position to spread awareness of environmental concerns because he thinks that everyone has a part to play in protecting the environment.

Shaun is not just creative in fashion and music. Along with acting, he has made a few film and television appearances. Even though acting differs from skating and snowboarding, Shaun relishes the challenge of taking on many personas and narrating tales via his performances. Shaun's acting adds another dimension to his already varied profession and lets him explore a different aspect of his creativity.

Shaun has achieved success, yet he never loses his gratitude or humility. He is grateful for all of his chances and the individuals who have helped and encouraged him during his journey. Shaun is a brilliant athlete and a great guy because of his humility and thanks.

His personal life is equally exciting and motivating off the rink as it is on. Shaun has an enthusiastic and upbeat approach to life, which is demonstrated by his activities, which range from founding businesses and giving back to the community to performing music and traveling. He demonstrates to us the value of pursuing our passions, maintaining our curiosity, and changing the world. His story serves as a helpful reminder that life is an adventure and that we should make the most of it.

CHAPTER 10: INSPIRING THE NEXT GENERATION

Shaun White's narrative embodies resilience, tenacity, and a resolute faith in his aspirations. When a small child gazed at the snow-covered mountains, he would see a playground full of limitless opportunities rather than just cold and ice. That boy's name was Shaun, and he had a passion for snowboarding and skateboarding as pure as the sunlight reflecting off of newly fallen snow at an early age.

Shaun grew up in San Diego, California, where there were sandy beaches and pleasant weather all around. Shaun, however, was more drawn to the adrenaline of skateparks and ski slopes than he was to the beach. At the age of six, he took his first snowboarding steps—more like slides—with the help of his family. Soon after, his skill started to become apparent.

Shaun had a difficult road. He had several difficulties, one of which was a heart ailment that needed surgery when he was a newborn. But these setbacks only strengthened his resolve. He put a lot of effort into his training, spending many hours honing his stunts and becoming an expert skateboarder and snowman. His perseverance paid off, and he soon started to distinguish himself in contests.

Shaun first saw the renowned skateboarder Tony Hawk when he was seven years old. Hawk saw Shaun's potential and gave him mentoring. Shaun started to succeed in amateur events with Tony's help and his unwavering determination. His goal was to be the greatest in the world, and he understood that would require reaching unprecedented, both material and symbolic altitudes.

At the age of thirteen, he got his big break in snowboarding. He competed against older, more seasoned competitors, and he overcame his nerves. Rather, he fueled his performance with his enthusiasm and energy. The snowboarding community took notice of his audacious stunts and bold demeanor. He became known as "The Flying Tomato" because of his amazing abilities and vivid red hair.

His love of skating and snowboarding didn't fade as he got older. He persisted in pushing the envelope of what was conceivable. He rose to fame with his daring acrobatics and original tricks that astounded onlookers. But more than his technical prowess, it was his attitude that motivated a lot of others. Shaun never failed to make people laugh, smile, and inspire others to pursue their goals.

Shaun experienced a pivotal moment during the Winter X Games, a prominent championship dedicated to extreme sports. He demonstrated his dominance in snowboarding and skateboarding by winning gold medals in both disciplines. His triumphs didn't end there. Shaun proceeded to participate in the Winter Olympics, where he triumphed in the halfpipe event many times. His performances were legendary, displaying not just his physical prowess but also his bravery and inventiveness.

There was more to Shaun's accomplishment than just medals. The goal was to encourage people to follow their ambitions, no matter how large or little, and to have faith in themselves. He demonstrated that everything is achievable if one has perseverance, hard effort, and an optimistic outlook. Shaun was a hero to younger skateboarders and snowboarders. He illustrated how the road to achievement is not always clear-cut, full of detours and occasional falls. But what distinguishes a great champion is getting back up and giving it another go.

Additionally, he gave back to the community by using his platform. He supported organizations that assisted underprivileged people and children by being involved in a variety of humanitarian endeavors. Not only did he wish to improve the globe, but also the slopes and skateparks. His generosity and kindness strengthened his standing as a source of inspiration for many.

Shaun continued to inspire the next generation even when he moved on from competitive athletics to other endeavors like music and entrepreneurship. He emphasized to everyone that living is about pursuing your hobbies and finding happiness in all that you do. Shaun's tale shows that the options are unlimited, whether one chooses to establish a new business, play an instrument, or do feats on a snowboard.

Shaun is still a well-known character in the sports community even after giving up on snowboarding and skateboarding competitions. He still serves as a source of motivation for young athletes worldwide. His legacy includes the spirit of adventure and the conviction that aspirations may come true in addition to the medals and records he achieved.

Shaun White's career inspires children who aspire to be skateboarders or snowboarders by demonstrating that anybody can succeed if they have the drive, tenacity, and guts to take risks and follow their dreams. His narrative inspires us all to dream large, to welcome difficulties, and to reach beyond the horizon. He will always be known as The Flying Tomato, who reached new heights and touched our hearts while demonstrating that everything is possible if you have guts and perseverance.

CONCLUSION

Shaun White is an incredible athlete who has motivated countless young people to follow their aspirations. Shaun, who went by the nickname "The Flying Tomato" because of his red hair, demonstrated that everything is achievable with perseverance and hard effort. Shaun used to love skiing and skateboarding as a child. He practiced for hours on end, falling a lot but always getting back up. His hard work paid off as he emerged victorious in both sports, taking home several trophies and accolades.

Shaun's path wasn't always straightforward. Despite obstacles and disappointments, he never gave up. He forced himself to hone his abilities and pick up new techniques. Shaun became one of the world's greatest athletes because of his bravery and inventiveness.

His goal was not just to triumph but also to encourage others to take risks and be bold.

Shaun is a hero to a lot of teenage skateboarders and snowboarders. They witness his enjoyment of life and his fervor for his work. Through Shaun's tale, kids learn that with hard effort and self-belief, they too can do great things. He tells children that they should follow their passions with all of their hearts.

Shaun White's influence extends beyond his amazing feats and gold medals. He demonstrates to them that if they are prepared to work hard and stay focused on their objectives, dreams may come true. His advice is very clear: constantly aim for excellence, be fearless, and never give up. Young athletes of the future will continue to be motivated to pursue their goals and aim high by Shaun's legacy.

QUIZ TIME!

1. What new activity did Shaun White try on a trip to Big Bear Lake?

A) Surfing

B) Skateboarding

C) Snowboarding

D) Biking

2. How did Shaun feel about snowboarding when he first tried it?

A) He found it easy

B) He was scared and gave up

C) He thought it was boring

D) He found it thrilling and challenging

3. What helped Shaun improve his snowboarding skills?

A) Practicing tricks from skateboarding

B) Watching videos of top snowboarders

C) Spending hours on the slopes

D) All of the above

4. Who was Shaun White's hero and inspiration for snowboarding?

A) His coach

B) His dad

C) His older brother, Jesse

5. How old was Shaun when he entered his first snowboarding competition?

A) Five

B) Six

C) Seven

D) Eight

6. What was one of the most memorable competitions for young Shaun?

A) The Winter Olympics

B) The Junior Nationals

C) The X Games

D) His first local competition

7. How many Olympic gold medals did Shaun White win in total?

A) Two

B) Three

C) Four

D) One

8. Where did Shaun White win his first Olympic gold medal?

A) Pyeongchang

B) Sochi

C) Turin

D) Vancouver

9. Besides sports, what other interest does Shaun White pursue?

A. Painting

B. Music

C. Acting

D. Writing

10. What nickname did Shaun White earn because of his long red hair and aerial tricks?

A. The Red Rocket

B. The Flying Carrot

C. The Speedy Tomato

D. The Flying Tomato.

Made in the USA
Middletown, DE
18 December 2024